Cornerstones

Cornerstones

Written by Danielle Bechtloff

Artwork by Danielle Bechtloff

ISBN: 9798498860923

Instagram: @firesrenditions

Publication Date: 10/20/2021

First Printing: 2021

Kindle Direct Publishing

Front Cover Stock Image: Shutterstock.com – ekosuwandono (Artita Studio)

Artwork: Danielle Bechtloff

@firesrenditions

Dedication: ded·i·ca·tion
(noun)
1. The quality or purpose of being dedicated or committed to a task or [higher] purpose
2. The action of dedicating a building or church
3. The words with which a book or other artistic work is dedicated.

Similar to: inscription, blessing

From Latin *dedicare* - 'devote, consecrate'

---

*This book is dedicated to the **broken**, the **helpless**, and the **lost**. It is for those who wander, wonder, the dreamers, those who feel out of place, and those who feel an intense longing for what seems unattainable, for the unexplainable. It's dedicated to those that have felt cornered, those who have been in positions of not having a choice or a voice.* ***May you always find your way back home, guided, even through the darkest night.***

"You will forget your misery;
you will remember it as waters that have passed away.
And your life will be brighter than the noonday; its darkness will be like the morning.
And you will feel secure, because there is hope; you will look around and take your rest in security.
You will lie down, and none will make you afraid..."

- Job 11: 16-19

It was all for you in seeds...

"Lost again
Broken and weary
Unable to find my way
Tail in hand
Dizzy and clearly unable to
Just let this go

I am surrendering to gravity and the unknown
Catch me heal me lift me back up to the sun
I choose to live

I fell again
Like a baby unable to stand on my own
Tail in hand
Dizzy and clearly unable to just let this go

High and surrendering to gravity and the unknown
Catch me heal me lift me back up to the sun
I choose to live, I choose to live, I choose to live—"

'Gravity' by A Perfect Circle

Contents

I.

II.

III.

IV.

V.

Merci: mer·cy

(noun)

French for *thank you*

1. an expression of one's gratitude

Merci ...

To the Divine Source and the sources of inspiration, those who have taught me valuable lessons, those who have shown me the beauty of life, those who pick me up after I fall [apart], and those who have supported and encouraged me - each enhancing the beat and blessing the ink. *Thank you for the lessons.*

Thank you beyond the convention of words.

I.

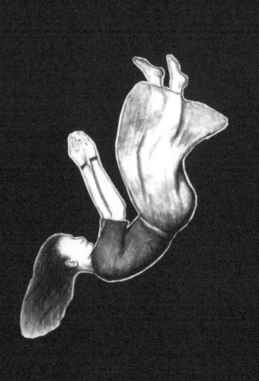

<u>ex nihilo</u>
(the falling of the drop, like ink to a blank page.)

silence.

        inhale

first breath

         exhale

                the beat

eyes opened

first sound, first cry

creation's core

             encore's applause

                         death rattle

                   last sound, last cry

                   eyes shut

                        inhale

                 last breath

                       exhale

                 silence.

crash landings

By the sea, time goes by
The seasons change & some will die
In places where none should be found
A place where hate & love are all around
Concrete beds & cigarettes
Congregations broken by misunderstandings
Somehow surviving, crash landings
Open wounds, the drugs consume
And leave little room to escape
This is the gypsy camp by the sea
Was once my fate—

XXI

A winter that felt like summer
Lived on a cliff facing the sea
In a shabby house that fell on me
Didn't take long to fall in love with the town
Didn't take long to constantly want Bobby around
A surfer with charm, a surfer with wit
Took a bite and realized this was it

Salad talks & endless walks
The sea with a pull like the sun's
Sang lullabies to her,
Her power would shun
No walls, always moving floor
No ceiling but stars
Back and forth on the boulevard
Didn't have much, but much was enough
Gained a few scars and the town made me tough

Harpoons & hiatus moons
Greeting gypsies with, "this place and this night are so strange,"
They'd laugh and say something like, "child, it's always this way"

Bobby showed me the ropes
And we talked and we smoked
A diverse range of people that stayed or they passed
Music made most nights
With the sea's cacophony crash
Making flowers from the leaves of palm trees
A time in life so familiar
So free

<u>the tempest</u>

the tempest whispers in his ear,
  "a little more
    remove your fear"
      fuller, fuller, nearly full
        twitching fingers pinch and pull

the tempest whispers once again,
  "don't stop now
    fill to the brim"

before he knows it, nothing's left
the tempest whispers,
  "you can fill
    more i bet"

DNR

Arrangements of numbers and letters
Placements of least to what's better
They know better
They always know better
Waiting for punch lines
Waiting in vain
Waiting for the formula to numb the pain
Falling out
Black feet
Needing chain breakers
Craving what causes the craving
No need for saving
We're aching
Fall out again

                                        DNR, near the end

Huffing, puffing, pushing in further
Fall out again

                                        DNR, near the end

Huffing, puffing, pushing in further
Fall out again

                                        DNR, near the end

Flat lines
Seizing what seizes our souls
Seize out, fall out
Tones of black
Line still flat
Forgetting where we're at

futility

I can't see myself
  It's dark and I don't understand
    The air is still
      And so am I
        My mind isn't

I'm confused
  Why can't I make the right move?
    At what point are things
      Passed the point of no return?

Will I ever be dragged out?
  Even when the answers are
    Clear the path isn't

How much can one take
  Before they fade
    Before they lose themselves
      Lose their minds
        Lose their lives

Where has strength gone?
My weaknesses
Crashing upon me

the faint

cracked and scrambled eggs
static mind, body, and spirit
in and out of tense
in and out of sense
rug swept from under

rattled
shattered illusions
scattered

seeing stars
taken breath
tingling limbs
ringing ears
inky black

internal earthquakes
sweeping
shocking shock waves
unbeknownst
loss and departures

rattling
shattering
scattering

thresholds

<u>kairos</u>

Bullet dodged
My impulse threatening me
It's heavy
It grazes my infected ear
Hear ringing of relief
So close to tragedy
I needed remedy
I ached for what betrays me

<u>four-points</u>

'for her own safety,' they said face straight
as they simultaneously locked the front gate
too many days of uninviting four-point restraints

tranquilized, such a heavy dose
exposed
relinquish control

because they said so

where did her freedom go?

<u>straitjacket</u>
quartered, she feels the pressure
held in or let out, for good measure

the straitjacket squeeze
ache for relief

release

oil
                    vinegar
ineffable forces
big bang proportions
'for her own safety' running its courses

seaside monologues

I'm talking to myself again
Pacing enthusiastically,
Flooding frustration

Take my warmth and
Shoes once more
Trying to take my
Soul with them

I'm talking to myself again
Eyes burning,
Barefooted again

The city pulls just like the tides
It listens as I find myself
Treading on its grounds

Castles on the other side
Infinite fish bowl on mine

I'm talking to the fish again
Explaining death but
Intending to save them
I didn't

The ocean breathes shallow, heavy
The Moon plays her disappearing act again
I'm talking to them both again
They whisper and they sing

go ahead

Welcome to seclusion
Where your whole world becomes a lie, delusion
Chronic fluorescence, constant light
Overwhelming loneliness, no one in sight
Don't say a word
Only other cells to be heard
Three meals, three walls, one door
Sleeping on a slab or the cold floor
Still hear the sound of the sea
Scared you'll never be free

Anything, anything, anything, anything

<u>just passing through</u>

i had a dream i was dead
as i slept in my concrete bed
a young boy led me through
saw some passed past people i knew
so briefly i asked,
"have i passed on or am i just passing through?"
walking by a lengthy mirror
the boy said,

                              "yes, you're dead here"

<u>encaged</u>
the life you could have had
is where hell resides
the lies we tell ourselves
to keep us alive
comfortable chaos & sweet entropy
we are encaged, we dream
to be free

pre-façades

I like to walk in places I don't belong
I reek of poverty
I walk around the
Super corporation get-everything-you-don't-really-need-store
And act like I'm not who I am

I have nothing to buy things with
But I pretend and talk to strangers
A beautiful ballet
My façade
Who knew I could act?

lull

As the storm lulled at the horizon
I called out your name
Sudden summer rain
Yet you vanished as quick as lightning's strike
Unfound I call out into the stormy night

I hear the evening's thunder
As I wonder
About the rain upon your skin
As I curse myself
For the very fear
Of letting you back in

winter's curse

Shivering through
Another storm
Craving warm
Anything for warm
Who was I then
Waiting for another storm to end
So many leeks
Days felt like weeks
Our backs hurt more than fists
Unchecked boxes on my lists
The storms, the heavy rains
Felt so cold upon my scarred skin
Unread letters
In waste bins
Icy veins
Few complaints
Frostbitten rains
Who even notices the pain?

<u>slipped hands in a crowd</u>

Shattered my peace of mind, pieces of the peace
Mangled, left at the threshold

And I'm let right on down
Again
No way in this state can one claim a win
And I'm let right on down
Again

Polaric shifts
Catastrophic rifts
Lost, but at what cost?
Found, the boldness fades soft

pining

Running back to the pines
Every time, every time
See more cars go passing by
Can't decide if I should try -

Running away from the pines
Seeing symbols and signs
Crawling from the darkness deep
It still haunts me in my sleep -

The pines are a confusing place to be
Lost lovers, lost lock and key
So aimless, no direction to be found
Although away, the pines I am bound -

<u>stumble</u>

Staggering, stumbling
Down lit barren streets
Loaded, no direction
No home to return to
No one in sight
Everything crashing upon you
You stumble on further

Still going—

<u>arrow's flight</u>

It's evenings like these I am pulled each way
Why is absence of our foundations?
Dazed desperate searching for
The motions I am battered,

I aimed the arrow straight
The moving mark
The arrow's flight a distance towards

loaded

How many shots does it take before
A.) You realize it's a mistake
   or
B.) Fate takes your place

Which choice will you make?

Either way,
It's a dangerous game
   or
Rhythmic ballet
It ends the same though
Sometimes quick
Sometimes slow
Deep down you know
But also you don't

The answer's clear
Especially with the end near
So which choice will you make?
How many is plenty?

ramps

I was looking for home
Usually walked all alone
A place few dared to tread
Late at night
Tried to destroy it all with my mind out of spite

Spent so much time searching
Spent so much time hurting
Spent so much time learning

I can still feel
I can still feel it all
As I forget–

ghosts

I am a product of a combination of misdirections
My brain tricks my surroundings
And my surroundings trick my brain
I am insane, but can you tell?
In this state I fell
"*This is our love!*" they're screaming
Strange rendition of a hopeless condition
Here's their intention
There's your injection
There's our infection
Here's this uneasy state

How many of us stuck in the daze
The haze
Of hell
But can you tell?

(*Whoever takes me to Heaven...*)

Striving, desperate reach for diminished doubt
My misunderstandings seem to scream so loud
What for, what's this about?

Just has to be

I suppose, what's will without free?
(But not completely, thankfully)

My faith, it shakes
Feel the depth of lessons that felt like mistakes
But why can't I grasp why it happens this way?
How to understand what I can't remember or comprehend
Despise the selfishness self demands
Ghosts misted in smoke
Forgotten, passed off like a bad joke
The faceless seem to be pulling the strings

Things are rarely as they seem
We'll see what tomorrow brings

<u>the passage</u>

In the pines,
through the passage of
weeping willows

Forgotten forget-me-nots
each wind   *(the ache)*
your bones remember

Sacred shivers
barren blessings
yawning through
death rattles
in baby's breath
life's smell of death

tangled

the energetic entanglement
caught in a moment, mindless in a moment
my mind went somewhere else
tangled mess
we've been here before
powerless
this infliction belongs to me
i need to see it separately
my mind went somewhere else
couldn't even feel the fear
shame detangling
disengaging

I'm swallowing sand as the sands are swallowing me whole
I'm sinking
Eyes full of sand, blinded
Wasn't I asleep?
Reaching for solid ground
I finally find my foundations

<u>unleash</u>

chaotic circles chronic
going nowhere faster
than the speed of light

dwell in the bottom
painting it gold

watch it fall apart
                    fall together
what to expect
when there's fading expectations

nothing left
resolve or entropy
acquiring acceptance
breaking patterns
acclimating
approaching
addressing
adjusting
                    accordingly

let me
show me
redirect my purpose
     my passion
     my direction
     my pursuits
don't let me fall again
don't let me get distracted
by the anglerfish's light
lead not into temptation

empty
     misled
         used
              betrayed
                   blamed

i feel things changing though
the shifting gears and catharsis
clarity
removing my insanity
i hope i learn from my mistakes
i hope i never again frequent this place

lighthouse

Won't find a home in the faux
Unnatural flow

Still I hope

I'll come back,
        refine,
            grow

Mislead me to my epiphanies
Abundance of countless crises:
Existential, quarter-life, dis ease of identity
Losing self, myself, am I the same as me?
What I want and what I need

Mental breakdowns, broken down,
Fruitlessly bound
Loss,
    loss,
        loss
Disappoint, searching, unfound
Ground Control, I'm so alone
Feeling owned, yet on my own
Lost at home
            Lost at home

I refuse to die
I'll at least try for paradise
I'd prefer to fly than lie
Until I land
And better understand
Hard to be me in the faux
Forgetting what I know
Approaching, passing an evolving threshold
Proof is in the pudding
Putting in endless exhaust towards lonely futility

Asking God for humility
Grace me with clarity
Not into faux, hard to me
Not my essence
Disinterest, indifference
Came and went

I won't stay lost in the mist
Lighthouse, guide me through this
I won't stay lost in the mist,
Lighthouse, guide me through this

II.

red stains on crisp, white bed sheets

pressure during a confession
need more pressure
need more confession
gazing for hours
flipping victims or explanations
one can never be too sure
layers of flesh, filéd
like your onion tattoo

how could you?

<u>wounded</u>

Bleeding in the Sahara
White sheets still
Getting redder
Never better
Never better

<u>black</u>

her eyes were black
the impact,
blame the hits or perhaps the smack
adorable yet adorning bruises and wounds
silently suffers tyranny, his anger consumes
could not speak
positioned always as weak

she rose above the beatings
better beckoned,
she reckoned
there must be more
and so she found herself forgetting days spent so degraded
so humiliated
released from the daze

enough

Just to see things clearly
Clinging dearly
Don't know what else to expect
Just yet, just yet

This is taking so much
Too much
It's never enough
When is enough?

Had enough again
Had enough again
Had enough again

I'm not enough again
I'm not enough again
I'm not enough again

Will it ever be enough?

<u>sons</u>

fatherly love
disguised
by bruise
close contact
despite no contact

disdain, contempt
malice
his wrath between
two faces, mistaken and mistake

he's never gone forever

do they see?

chop her down
indulge in her
core's sap

the reverb
        of her
bare, but not barren   footsteps
in the rain

<u>muted</u>

As my top lip bleeds, I take a walk
We play it off
You inject into yet another
To the ones you call sister and brother
Who has fallen at your hand?
Especially in this hazardous land

I crave to be special
I crave to be found
Special and found
Sleeping on the ground
Weeping for what remains unchanged
Unmoved
Deranged

Injecting toxicity
I crave to be special

beastly brutes
Scratching my head, glued to the sidewalk at the crossing point

reap

"Stay away from me!"
        To the nth degree,
       Her at three,
       Her at fifteen,
See the unseen

Peeling layers of stained,
Tattered remnants
Out of guilty, lies-through-grinning-teeth defendants
Here is their happy ending

                     Here

Shown sheer
Reaching for the rear view mirror

boa

can't

                                 breathe

boa
    constrictor

reach for
           anything
                 anything to take in

cornered again
desperation
  ink poured
    creeping
     chronic

take it all in
on release—

<u>strangled</u>

i know i take your breath away
but how could you take mine?
what is the price of sacrifice
to take another's time?

<u>eclipse</u>

they whispered, "my moon, the world would not be without you-"

<u>dread lock</u>

the walls screamed,

no mercy

but she did not

and turned to stone

<u>echoes</u>

her restrained body
her unrestrained screams
echo endlessly

                                                her restrained body
                                             her restrained screams
                                                    echo endlessly

unwelcomed corners

skittish
two for flinching, clenching
stand tall
when you feel small
cower, cover
from a lousy lover
stand tall
when you feel small
don't like how low
i can feel from such force

from small

i grew

post-fall

i flew

softly, softly

Softly speak
petals to my
center

Oldest offer
light steps on
earth

Fleeting flicker
warming out and
in

Tiny thunder
humming into my
existence

<u>the give & take</u>

she sighed *maybe*
hope nearly extinguished

<u>the darkest night</u>

she heard the wind whisper, "you too, knew the bullet's paths"
lightest traces of the aftermath

her silence
unlike any weapon known
piercing
such intensity in the undertone

his double-edged tongue
the severest slice
paper cuts
the sharpest knife

this night has been so dark
so long
why do we insist on ignoring right
rewarding wrong?
holding our breath for the approaching dawn

dancing with shadows longing for once was
ashes to ashes
dust to dust
the wind will take us

amongst ashes
the flames find themselves
burning bright
even through the darkest night

<u>mercy</u>

I won't beg you for mercy
I won't beg you

I won't crawl before you
I won't live on my knees
I won't beg for your scraps
I won't beg you

I won't starve without your scraps
I won't beg you

eyes wide shut

in a corner of a cell i felt you
screaming in my face
my inner child between us,
filling me with grace

she showed you through each
tortured wall
a warrior standing, still
so
small

the piercing reverb shook you,
the stream of regret
she & i walked together
away as the sun set

<u>a haunted farewell</u>

haunted by a woman
that loved you, what for?
farewell with a
final walk out the door
last glimpse of a back
of a woman not looking back
response to his vicious attack
not a word she said
as her nose bled red
the door closed as
he first felt regret
but
not enough
to persuade, he ignores the pain
yet haunted he will remain—

legion

The walls were closing in
Back to the wall
I'd rather be back to back
Know my back is had as a fact
Enforcing your power
Taking all in your path
I'll pay it forward by empowering the powerless
I'll take your submission
The sound of my laugh at the aftermath
Mark my words
Left a mirror and left

Counting paper cuts
Spill your guts
Have you the guts to face your self?
The mirror is beckoning
For your confrontation
Come get to know your own creation
Pieces of your intentions
Reflections

There's nowhere you can hide
It's your shot and you seem to be drawing a blank
Turn your internal combust into a combustion engine
I set myself on fire

From the Source

No more pain
No more blame
No more shame

For the love of all that's left
The best that's yet to manifest

I choose to live

The sound of ignition
From the floor to floored
The unloading
Cosmic proportions

Come back with a legion

69

III.

disturbing the peace

Walking by lakes without ever seeing them
Traffic passes, half-mast flags and losing wars
On borrowed time, determining what is mine,
What is ours, what are they?

Even though we feign interest in conversation
Eluding the emphasized conflicts that
Devour us daily
Show up to service early
Choking on coffee
Aching feet
Melted wax on concrete
What should we be doing?

Overnight construction
Questioning and wandering
It's concerning

Tracing forever on lumpy arms
And fingering holes where teeth once were
Selecting and processing information
Adding to taste, still aimless
Straining what's left
Popping blood vessels
Sharing second choices, sacrificial sentence
It's endless

Unrealistic pursuits
Dreams trapped in bottles
And remnants of last night in dirty newspaper
Fixated on beliefs that may change
Like channel surfing
Are you so sure?

Fluctuating and swaying, karma only
How we want for ourselves
Still we soak up and eat information
With no basis and see that as so
Walls built to block out, eclipse
Intolerant and still repeating
What fails
Scared of change yet always changing
Always moving yet unmoved

We are desensitized, unimpressed
Angry over small matters and numb to what does
What can we do?

Displaced, needles in arms
Buzzed on indifference
Unaffected, unexplainable, undivided

Naked in cold cells
Fermenting, fevered by confusion
Denied, in denial
"Can you spare..."
No, no, I need this more
I need this now
You need not

Carving their words on our bodies
Splattered walls and splattered streets
Disturbing the peace
Staring, unmoved into sadistic eyes
Staring into, staring through
Bullets in stares
Discomfort, shifty sinking paranoia
Watch me, watch me
Watching
Look to left, look to right

Indicating what's right
Follow my formula
We and they
Who's to say?

Herded and chasing
Making coffee, sweeping, scratching, forgetting
Still what matters to me
What matters to most?

Crossing paths
Signing illiterately
Re-reading and contemplating methods
Full closets, arm bones under doors
Forks in sockets
Banishment and directions to doors

Exit here
Enter here

<u>shoot here</u>

War on their name
Pain is their game
Brain trained
Licensed, plagued with
Disturbed sleep

Still I weep

When it comes
Signed their soul
Younger than sin
Trust the ones who threw them in
A hero to some
An enemy to some
Their restless soul
Their conscience unresolved
Were they wrong?
Were they right?
Will they ever know?
Obligated to fight
Protecting
It's conflicting

Still I weep

<u>seventeen dollars</u>

Seventeen dollars flashed on the cracked screen of the ATM
He coughed, popped a pill, thought,
Maybe I could pull out more than ten

Before he could even comprehend the next move to make,
Before he even got to take what seemed to be a mistake
In the reflection of the cracked screen he saw the flash of a mask

Before he knew it, the mask asked, or more of a bark with a spit,
"This is it. Give me what's mine, I want it all, not a bit.
You've got five before this cracked screen is nothing more than your skull.
Don't make a move, other than your fingers or my fingers on the trigger I'll pull—"

He looked at the cracked screen, seventeen dollars flashed anxiously
He had a lighter and a cigarette in reach
Lit one up and started to speak,
"I've done a lot of time,
Twenty-four years to be exact
And I've probably lost my mind
Not probably, I'd say in fact,
In places you probably wouldn't believe
In places I couldn't leave
And when those locked doors finally swung and I could walk more than eight feet
No other feeling could ever really compete
Where even looking at your mask is more inviting than empty walls
I'd give you more than the seventeen dollars I'm not quite sure I can pull out
Have a cigarette, what's this really all about?"

The mask blinked twice,
Reached for it, but something didn't feel right

The mask looked around, lit the cigarette, let out a subtle sigh said,
"You don't know me, what I've been through in my life—"

He looked at the cracked screen,
Rubbed his tired eyes
Heard a passing siren go by
Let out a tired reply,
"Look,
Life's the longest thing we ever do, but it's so short it passes fast. What
were you thinking of doing after the swift seventeen dollars no longer
lasts?
After this I was about to head home, it's just six blocks, why don't you
walk with me, we'll pour some drinks and maybe we could talk"

The mask took a last drag and felt compelled to walk with the man
He felt a weight lifted off of him
As he shook the man's calloused hand
The cracked screen blinked seventeen dollars as they headed the other
way
A lesson that's worth more than any priced pay, any day

<u>the muses</u>

I crave the caress of the muses
It fuses
My sometimes seemingly spiraling spirit
Whispers in my ear, do my best to mirror

Sometimes ink seeps deeper than you'd think

poetic justice

Poetic justice is the phenomena felt in every cell
It's even felt in the niches of the depths of Hell
It's felt in every corridor of the seas
Brings warriors to their knees
It's carried whispers in the morning breeze
It causes a halt
A jolt
A pause
Can't be ignored
It gnaws, it claws
The core
The raw
Might cause you questioning everything you ever saw
It's a polite subtle knock
And has the power to destroy locks

Doesn't impose, just makes its presence known
You can't help but feel its poetic justice
Feel the resonance, sets precedence
Can't be denied
Gives the cosmos a reprieve for a needed sigh

Vessels of muse
Entropy ensues, unglues
Realigns, stops before it consumes

Artists in dimly lit quarters and spaces
Expressing, stating, relating, portraying
And sometimes complicating the status quo
Gets you to question what you know
Artist statements that open doors, open eyes, unveil real lies
Compelling souls to rise

<u>remnants</u>

vital drops
struck with your strokes
pieces of your peace
of your intentions
reflections

<u>hung</u>
his heart is the heaviest part of this tree—

triple goddesses

she went to his grave every morning and wept upon his bed
tears woven with the land
her daughter, upon acquainting [inherent] grief, every afternoon would
weep upon his bed
as would her daughter, familiarizing intrinsic sorrow, weeping every
evening
the land impregnated by their lamentations

graveyard of dreams

He is the keeper of the Graveyard of Dreams
Fills each plot with dirt,
He does not feel its hurt
Knows every spot, has Sundays off
Has been there thirty-two years
It's watered with so many tears
Calloused hands, they now shake severe
One afternoon the ground rattled, shook worse than his hands
He put on his glasses, smudged, to see what he couldn't understand
Each stone, each now no longer engraved
Except the word 'Saved'

IV.

sighing sea
oh in the ways
    the waves
               my emotions
                      the motions
    how they move
    how they break
    how they make
             me
             me

crash
    come back
[de]part
faces deep
celestial castration

(please) don't go
           so soft
(please) don't go
           so soft
you are home
           so bold
you are home
           so bold

hold on
hold hope
new day
please stay

sighing sea
your many voices
pieces of me, we
lyrical verses of us
our verses and versus'

expressing
the formless

                           with   without

every corner of the world

Two stars collide
From different sides
Explosive each direction
Adoration as the latest infection
Frozen, motionless, time stands still
Each breath held until
Breeze of relief
No ounce of grief
At least until things resume

First meet of bride and groom

sunday talks & gully walks

If they try to take me away
Promise you will keep me safe
Promise we will find a way
Promise you will stay

Stung by stinging nettle
Gully walks
Sunday talks
Itchy legs
Sunday dresses
Sunday gully walks

<u>drops</u>

how lovely is the fall of love
unexpected gifts from above
the fall brings wings
God's grace sings,
"I made this one for you"

<u>shred</u>

counting paper cuts
the shattered glass
dissolves into the passing past

causality

rarely well-received
reminders of what we truly need
such a simple mission
blesséd to be given
so much a blur
for her

motion repeats
causality meets
intense rattles
once severe battles

dissolve
reverse
traverse
unveils and lifts the curse

he seems to be in everything
it was all for you in seeds

<u>the waltz</u>

How the room would feel
From their presence alone

Undeniable, undoubtedly
Sheer loveliness shown
Time stands still
each
exchanged
glance

Each encounter enveloping adoration's trance

They dance around
The room
They grow,
They are in bloom

<u>midnight sun</u>

she came down the mountain

always beside me,
humble midnight sun,
my beloved bringing forth
(what i had left)

and cried amen–

revere

midnight sun
midnight moon
duets
entangled cords
highways for life
harmonic disposition
complementary composition
weaving the tides with lavas churn

birth pains, sighs of relief
from the cosmos
clearing the cobwebs
burping residual
                                        creation's core
sending subtle sensations

push
pull
fill to full
the ebbs
the flows
the waxes
the wanes

dial's rotating
    to deliver
                kingdom's coming

                                        cry in the wilderness

passion

let me impassion you.
fill you with fervor.
aflame.
apex unending.
ardor.

yours.

mind, body, spirit
                on fire
                  Δ

hum softly into
whisper's rendering petals
silent resonance

this tiny thunder
each tick of serenity
stillness in faint beat

ink

utter in the undertone
the inklings pool

the road -
our paper

you are the ink to my quill
rolling the roads in inkwell

<u>the sun is not dead</u>

walk in a room as the lights douse themselves, untouched
feel the earth shake alone
dog will have a bone
dog will have a home
the sun is not dead
feel the blood go to your head
the sun is not dead
the best is to happen yet

<u>birth of spring</u>

the world at once fell asleep
until the first red rose bloomed
through the remnants of snow

<u>sleeping in the garden</u>

sleeping in the garden
that we planted

the trees deeply rooted
they whisper in my sleep
the flowers hum of home
our home

i sway
in the light breeze
this night
ink

the moon placed peeking
between the leaves dancing

uprooted
to this garden
growing

i dream
clear
of our peace

<u>divine dew</u>

the morning dew
image bearing new
walk towards the sun
warm light upon my face
morning's like these
so full of grace

<u>bridges</u>

unread letters littered the floor
left a rose closer to nevermore   ***nevermore***
                                              clarity arising, arriving
what to say at the mouth of the river?
where it meets the sea
pieces of me
into the breeze
not an easy place to speak
two mountains flowing grace's bed
upon which i fell nearly dead
the chi of forty feet
the chi of forty feet
refining, enhancing my beat
falling to pieces, won't you follow me?
uplifted by angels, guiding
blesséd for the uplifts
graceful gifts
another imprint at a bridge
i chose to live
i walked a way
walking a way
walk a way
come walk with me

                                              walking along the sea
                                                          beating
oh in the ways
the waves
the motions of my emotions
the waves
the ways
with what's left, what's left to say?

V.

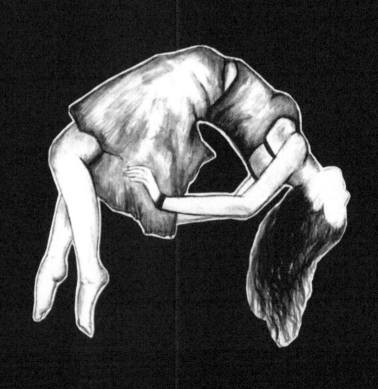

00

black birds songs long when midnight meets two zeros
freedom's hard to feel in cages, unsung heroes
from the distance, a free bird listens

left to lose,
tied, denied dreams
black birds cursèd
broken wings

tied
and broken feet
with a broken voice sings

sings of freedom

new dawn
new song
canticum novum
flight might come soon

<u>cornerstones</u>

Left off course kicking pine cones
Reacquainted, this time there must be acclimation
There must be
Feeling confusion beyond belief
Back to the sea
Was left hanging on the side of the cliff
This is really it
Was left hungered for more
One step closer to nevermore

I apologize from the cornerstone of my soul
Would turn each failure into gold
Conversations so direct turn into static
What's withheld, my mind's erratic
I don't like who I'm becoming
So sick of the running

Some nights it was so hard to find sleep
Found myself unable to speak
Couldn't process what to think
Trying to find my own voice
Be in the interest of good choice
Barriers, why can't we talk it out
Why ignore or scoff at my painful confusion and doubt
I'll set aside misblame
Try to through my processing pain

I apologize from the cornerstone of my soul
Would turn each failure into gold
Conversations so direct turn into static
What's withheld, my mind's erratic
I don't like who I'm becoming
So sick of the running

Here's to what's to come to growth from the painful places we have
known
I hope we both find what we need and spread vibrations of healing, the
attractive feelings
Unwind chaotic confusion
Express it in encouragement, relief from delusion
Aspire, inspire, gratitude in receiving inspiration
Our pain will find healing and honesty is worth admiration

I apologize from the cornerstone of my soul
Turn each painful presence into gold
Heal us both
Still I hope

chase

head pressed into nothingness
i'll walk away forever
hard to believe
there's one for me
who won't rip me to shreds
savour solitude
i'll **never** pine again
i'll walk away forever

relinquishing the chase

<u>naked light</u>

fell for an angel
 fell down
        down
            down
  and then fell apart, fell through
for things to fall into place
fell back on my saving graces
falling to me to fly

uplift   uplift
     uplift   uplift
          uplift
blessèd spiritual gifts
Truth of the spirit on your lips
remedy for the sick
pure elixir
positive solution
to transform the negating poisonous toxicity

new combination to create far greater

we're here for you
and will never leave you
never abandon Truth
sisters & brothers rise, pain let go
roses of the kingdom's garden
fear removed
forgotten misery, our dreams to be upon us
new beginnings for the broken
shining amongst the rough

<u>postcards</u>

in through the airwaves
out of the labyrinth, the enigmatic maze
time for a new phase

the sea speaks
hears the quiet weeps
of the delicate daughters and sons
hears the sentences run
chorus of the universe you feel underneath your skin
pictures inclusive we're all in

blur the edges expanding
no mind will ever be fully comprehending
the grandness, the majesty
even in the micro-debris of the sea

bījā

tiny seeds
the sustenance
resulted feeds
radiant visitations
initial recognitions

there it comes

there it goes
here

annihilation of doubts & fears

timely reactions
results
of unstoppable forces

inferno

let this fuel be your ignition
after the revival of your broken condition
set your soul ablaze
let the spark of your eye inspire your burning desire to light up the dark

such intensity from the flickers of your madness
hard not to stare at the fervent illumination of your amelioration
kindled by your compelling condition
like lightning's strike amongst the evening embers

rise from the ashes of [your own] destruction
dance with the flames
celebration of life after being nearly extinguished
dusky charcoal to fine-diamond
warm yourself with the heat of your passion
vanquish what blows out your incandescent nature
face to face with your inner critic,
set your fears ablaze
and release with the smoke—

<u>raving raven</u>

passionate movings
   defibrillate
      jump-starts
                   anew
reboot
r e a r r a n g e m e n t
   of dilated pixels

transform

and awaken gradually
to your ripples

compass rose

she glides weaving in corridors
that echo midnight musical mysticism
    her magic
bohemian spirit
rhythmic motions of untouchables
that cannot be destroyed
her energy lights this treaded street
                              beating
fueling the drawing
feeling towards relief, towards life itself
following subtle feelings
quiet whispers
compass rose
leading the strays
towards paradise

resonance

the sacred silent spaces between our thoughts
between sounds and speech
where poetry, music, and art are composed

                                              rhythm
                               the rhythmic ballet of life

the unspoken unveiling of the spirit
the cadence
the slightest soft whisper

                                              guiding

vibrations rising
tuning to the frequency of

                    ascension

                              transcendence

<u>fever frenzies</u>

passional electric energy
spirit's fuel
paroxysms uncontained
in cages created
            from unconsulted choices

lingering words above
                        the floor
                                never never, why what for?
anything anything
unlocked door

life's lessons
enlightening
enlivening

as life goes on

beaten breasts

uncorking the fermented wine of wrath
losing where we were once at
displaced welcome mat

cannot escape the light
was it truly worth the fight?

beating breasts
forthright overcomers admitting
self-proclaimed saints denying
humble turnovers
or comparisons and endless lying

trapped in the bottles of lies
while the righteous, the loving ascend
to inviting skies

<u>dulia</u>

silence in heaven
stillness; struck
unforgettable

revere the majesty
spirit's Truth speaks
to the meek
                    their inheritance

vindication established
the substances nourish
sincere desires for redemption
gifts received
upon maturity

heard word
meaning beaming
promised purpose
there you are

<u>uplift</u>

fallen angels fly the uncharted skies
they lead, returning
after the impact of falling flat
from breeze to shallow seas
stones in slingshots

lost beat restored

over the edge

resumed pulsation
their blood of divinity's consecrated cocktail
their cosmic ethereal wings cause waves of fervor
bravely triumphing despite chaos' brutal blows

raison d'être

rising

once helpless   unsung heroes
can no longer be ignored
no longer cornered
the holy whole
full
ripples

staying in the circle

cannot deny what is the essence of you

healing broken spirits
suffering shattered
fusing failures
mending misfortune
vengeance vanquished
simple twist of fate
                 fleeting
fickle change of fate's course
unexpected miracles
r e a r r a n g e m e n t
spreading
contagious mutations
of once hopeless despair
language of anguish muted

faint soft sighs
deepest gratitude praising towards

aurora

I came to
I have arrived
Wide-eyed
Oh the price for true eyes
Insight
Relief to finally see
So much beauty
The things that pass us by
Couldn't distinguish blur from lies
I felt my third eye cry
Oh the price to see the beauty of life

Seen the light of day
Seeing the spectrum of the waves
The shades

The sight of clarity
Catharsis, the real, the sincerity
Can finally perceive for myself the very remedy
Recognizing what I truly need
Seeing clear what was right in front of me

I came to
Can't believe what I was seeing
The gift of twenty-twenty whence before was out of sight
To see matters in the light

At least now I know
Grateful for the growth
Now divinely touched when to go
And go on
Discerning right from wrong
The too far the extreme the too much
So out of touch out of sight out of mind

I'd rather see eye to eye
Trying again after you tried
And knowing when to cut ties
Out of sight out of mind
The senses that I rendered
I came to—

<u>lost at sea</u>

the flight of your darkness
surpassed by the Light, shining
unexpected divine timing

the beacon beckons at the faint horizon in the distance
you squint, shift your hazy lens

once lost at sea, adrift
native to the abyss, oblivion, the void,

nothingness

abiding no longer
faith growing progressively stronger
emerging
course steered towards the Source

HOME

He took the bus
Thought of us
I wonder where we go
Wonder as we wander
Although never alone

She took the bus
Thought of us
I wonder where we go
Wonder as we wander
Although never alone

In 'we' we find our Home

They start as friends, then meet again
Can't help but hold her hand
A new light sheds once was
They just can't seem to give up

He's at the wheel
Waves of how he really feels
The light bursts through the cracks

She's at the wheel
Discerning faux from real
Can't help but feel the pull

They stay, they find their ways
A middle door, to balance the extremes

   Hope
Finding **Home** in we

<u>pilgrimage</u>

(in stride, **despite**)

Hope
    the beat that guides towards

    inhale
the
the
      exhale

the gracious graze of muse
of sweet Serenity
peaceful presence, so soft
the resonance

when i cannot see
when it's all so dark
Hope beckons the broken
          stumbling
          searching

Hope cradles the helpless
      lifts the fallen
under this wing, Divine Love
guarded
      carried

Hope moves my core
their mantras guide us Home

Made in the USA
Coppell, TX
24 November 2021

66323218R00092